Extraordinary Things Happen on Ordinary Days

Kathy Lark, Author and Compiler
Amanda Mills, Illustrator

Independently Published
Amazon/Kindle
ISBN: 9798296611819

Kathy Lark, Author
Amanda Mills, Illustrator

Holt Publishing 2025
HoltPublishing4U@gmail.com

FOREWORD

Kathy Lark, one of WGGS TV-16 television's faithful servants, makes us re-think our daily lives in this, her second book, *Extraordinary Things Happen on Ordinary Days*. How many of us miss what God wants us to see and/or experience because we feel that there is really "nothing special" about this "ordinary day"?

Often times we miss blessing upon blessing each and every day because, quite frankly, we are either not looking for, nor are we expecting, or we could possibly be out of step with the Lord.

From her time working with us at WGGS, Kathy has received many calls and prayer requests from faithful viewers during the day as a receptionist and a prayer partner. As she has listened to our views and noted their prayer requests, the Holy Spirit has given her great insight into the extraordinary things going on in individual lives on what they may even perceived to be an ordinary day.

In God's Kingdom we must EXPECT him to show us his handiwork and answers to our prayers and concerns, regardless how "ordinary" the day may seem.

Enjoy the reading!

— *Pastor Benny*
Pastor Benny Presents

DEDICATION

To my family, friends, and gifted writers.

FROM THE AUTHOR

Kathy Lark

"Fear thou not; for I am with thee: be not dismayed;
for I am thy God: I will strengthen thee;
yea, I will help thee; yea, I will uphold thee
with the right hand of my righteousness" (Isaiah 41:10).

TABLE OF CONTENTS

PREFACE

Some of our most unforgettable memories and events in our lives are the small things that happen every day. We rarely remember them as they get lost or forgotten with time and age. The reason for writing this book is to urge us to recall, while we still can, some of those seemingly insignificant, unforgettable events.

When we are living day-to-day life, we may not realize that we are influencing someone along the way. We never know who is watching our actions and mentally recording our deeds. We may be the pattern for their lives.

When researching for this book, my idea was to record our stories and preserve the many unique memories we all have. This book contains some of those stories. They are true stories about different people from all walks of life, both rich and poor, bond and free. These people have a story worth telling. The words will make you laugh, cry, and then ultimately realize how blessed we are just to read their stories. You may often wonder, like I do, why someone acts the way they do. Hopefully their own words will enlighten us.

Some have angel visitations, memories of tragic events, fond memories of family member that who have passed on, while some tell of their own healing experiences. All just want to share meaningful parts of their life with us. Everyone has a story.

I've been told there are many ways that angels make themselves known when they are around. Some say that if you find a feather in places near your home an angel has been there. Others say if you get a visit from a red bird, a loved one is near. Still others have dreams, see visions or have certain feelings come over them for no explainable reason. The reason for the feathers at the beginning of each chapter are to remind us that we have an angel that guards over us (Psalms 91:10-11).

As you read, put yourself in the writer's story, and see how they will come to life for you. Hopefully they will call to mind a special memory of your own. Some of the writers you may recognize and some not, but all will remind you that we serve a loving God who watches over us every day in many *extraordinary ways*.

Happy reading!
Kathy Lark

CHAPTER 1
God Listens

If you're anything like me, any project needs a confirmation from God so that we know His blessings are on it. When working on the writing of this book, I was beginning to doubt a little bit that it would ever get finished. I've always believed that a good book title was essential for encouraging people to pick up the book and read it. I knew that God had given me the title of the book in a dream. When the morning came, I felt the words were the right ones, but I was scared to voice the title to anyone. Trying to keep the title a secret from everyone until the book came out was a little bit of a challenge. The first questions that everyone wants to know is what's the title and what's it about.

On Mother's Day, May 11, 2025, I received my confirmation, two times. Kathy Lance, a wonderful, Christian lady that comes to our church to play the piano, sing and sometimes bring the Word to us, was speaking on this Mother's Day morning.

I was sitting on the pew thinking about the book and second guessing myself over the title. Kathy brought a great Word from God and was nearing the end of her sermon when out of nowhere she said to us. "You know God causes 'Extraordinary Things to Happen on Ordinary Days'".

That was the title of my book! I thought to myself, there is no way she just said that? Here I was still questioning God and fretting over the book title, yet at the same time He was giving Kathy the words to say that morning that would get my attention and settle my questioning. Not only did she say them one time, but after my rambling thoughts and denials, she repeated them again. "Always remember, 'Extraordinary Things Happen on Ordinary Days'". If this is not straight from God, I don't know what is. I absolutely got chills when she said the book title. Kathy knew nothing about the book, nor me even writing a book. We don't really know each other except in passing. But this day God sent her as a confirmation to me. Only God can give us God moments on God's time!

After church I went up to Kathy and told her what had just happened. We rejoiced together at God's ability to be right on time and to prove He knows what we need, even before we ask Him.

This book was still being written and now I know God has His signature on it. It is in God's hands and His will. It is time to publish it.

Many thanks to Kathy for hearing the Word and freely speaking it to others. She is a talented speaker and a God-send to our church family. I will never forget this Sunday morning service. Thank you Kathy and thank You God! God tells us in His Word, *"And they went forth, and preached everywhere, the Lord working with them, and confirming the word with signs following"* (Mark 16:20).

— *Kathy Lark*

CHAPTER 2
Keep the Power On

I am a widow now for 17 years. I live alone. I committed my life to Jesus at 25 years of age and never looked back. Prayer is my strength when I am weak and my prayer is refuge in times of trouble. Prayer is a language that many people don't understand. It is a language that's always available when we want to talk to God. We can talk to God just like we talk to our best friend, because He is our best friend. When I talk to God He never thinks I'm pitiful nor feels sorry for me. He is my best friend and I can tell Him everything.

When I think of prayer, I remember the story of Jesus asleep in the boat in Mark. His disciples are afraid and try to wake Him up because they believe the boat is sinking. When He arose He simply said to the wind "Peace be still." Immediately there was a great calm.

If you get real with God, He'll get real with you. He'll answer prayers sometimes in a way that you don't expect or not like you wanted them to be. Even some prayers are not answered at all (yet to be). Sometimes He takes us by the way of the potter's wheel. The potter knows how much pressure the vessel can take and how many times it needs to go around the wheel as the following song says:

13

But the Potter knows the clay.
How much pressure it can take.
How many times around the wheel.
'Til there's submission to His will.
He's planned a beautiful design,
But it'll take some fire and time.
It's gonna be okay.
'Cause the Potter knows the clay.

There are three special times that I know God has answered my prayers. The first one was when I was taking my mother to the doctor and another car ran a red light and t-boned us in the side. I went through the window. My legs were tangled in the steering wheel. I was covered with broken glass, but I had no broken bones and no stitches.

The second time was when we were moving out of a huge 20-plus room house. I was making my last trip to get my flowers to take to our new home. The old house had a long hallway that was not well lit. The only light was the light from the large windows in the front door. I was at one end of the hall and saw a shadow of a man coming toward me down the hall. He was a big man with a hammer in his hand. I began to back up but he kept coming. I kept saying in a strong, determined voice, "What are you doing here? You don't belong here." I felt God's presence and I was never afraid. The man kept coming and when he reached the back door, he just turned and went outside and walked away down the street.

The third time was when I had rheumatoid arthritis in my neck and back. I got to the point I couldn't do anything for myself. I had to be carried up and down the steps and had to be helped to feed myself. It had gotten to the point; the doctor was suggesting a wheelchair for me.

Many, many people prayed for my healing and as they prayed I kept remembering the scripture in II Corinthians 12:9 that talks about Paul's thorn in the flesh. "When I prayed God told me, "My grace is sufficient for thee."

When Dave, my husband, took the children to church one Wednesday night, I had a long talk with God. I told Him about my husband and children I had to take care of and church groups to help with and how I couldn't be in a wheelchair and do all that I had to do.

Dave came home and gave me my medicines and we all went to bed. The next morning I got up and decided to make coffee. I had no pain. I hadn't been able to do this in months. I woke Dave and told him God had healed me.

On my last visit to the doctor that day, I canceled all my doctor's appointments and told him I was healed and didn't need to see him anymore. I saw the same doctor several years later and he said I see you still don't need me. All this shows God does His best work in our weakness. He is always in control!

Dave's word from God was always trust. He trusted the Lord until the day he passed. In an unconscious state he spoke to God still declaring, "I trust you Lord."

Once when my friend's little boy prayed, he mentioned everyone he knew, he prayed for people he didn't know, he prayed for anything and everything he could think of. His prayer was being offered during a thunderstorm and as he was praying he said "Lord, please, please keep the power on." That should be our prayer every time. "Please, please, Lord, keep the power of the Holy Spirit on in our lives." God tells us, *"Now the God of hope fill you with all joy and peace in believing, that ye may abound in hope, through the power of the Holy Ghost"* (Romans 15:13).

— *Pam McElrath*

Just a personal footnote to this story...

I will never forget the first time we walked into Barton's Memorial Church. We decided to visit new churches to see if we might find a better fit. My father-in-law suggested Barton's Memorial, because when he was a young man this is where he attended. The first people to greet us there was Pam and Dave McElrath. This small congregation was just what we were looking for. We felt the love of the people and God as we entered the doors. The pastor, Reverend Otis Hopkins was a godsend. He always seemed to have the words God knew we needed to hear. We grew to love all the people at the church. Pam and Dave were instrumental in getting my husband, Noah, and I into regularly attending church. When we met Pam and Dave, we knew we were home. They were there when our daughters were born and later became our daughter's god-parents. Had we not met them when we did, I dare say we would have been in church at all. Pam and Dave shared the love of God, and the Holy Spirit really worked through them to reach us. We miss Dave tremendously and Pam is still our inspiration. Thank You God for Christians who know how to share Your love. And thank You Holy Spirit for keeping the power on.

—Kathy Lark

CHAPTER 3
God's Road Map

It was late winter 2024 when I saw an online challenge on Facebook called 40/40 challenge. It was a challenge to walk 40 miles in 40 days and with every step pray, listen to praise music or scripture. I have never been one to enjoy exercise, but I needed to get my body moving in order to be healthier and lose the last 25 pounds of my goal.

I started my walk in uptown Travelers Rest; partly because it's flat and partly because I would have to be intentional about doing it. I didn't walk the Swamp Rabbit Trail, but walked the sidewalks from the intersection of Sunrift Adventures to Travelers Rest Oriental, then up to Trailblazer Park and back. It was a good walk of about 1.5 miles per day. At the end of the 40/40 challenge I had walked 96 miles, all the while singing praise songs and praying for God to reveal to me the answer to my big question, "What's next?" I want more God so, "What's next?" After the challenge was completed I continued to walk my same path.

While going to Walmart for my groceries one day, on a whim, I applied for a job part-time in the online shopping department and I got the job. During my first few days, there was a young Hispanic girl who just gravitated towards me. She knew very little English and my Spanish is limited as well. Google translate works, but you have to be face-to-face to use it. We soon figured out that we could text one another and it would come to our device in our language.

She was also one of the employees who came in at 5:00 as I did and she had to walk to get there. I was concerned for her safety. I soon realized it was her house that I walked by while doing the challenge and praying.

Later I learned she had been through the horrific murder of her brothers at the hands of the police in her home country.

She is a single mother with a young daughter, Alexandra, with Down syndrome as well as leukemia. I took her and her daughter to doctor appointments and soon we became very good friends. She needed a workplace friend and God caused our paths to cross at just the right time.

The Lord sends us where we're needed and wants us to go, all we have to do is follow His lead. I feel that my life was forever changed by meeting Estephany and Alexandra. They are two angels that I met along life's path when I wasn't even sure what the right path for me was, but God knew.

The Bible tells us, *"In all thy ways acknowledge him, and he shall direct thy paths"* (Proverbs 3:6).

—*Tiffany Hughes*

CHAPTER 4
Pa's Prayers

I saw jars of "Grandma's Molasses" at a grocery store and purchased a jar of the dark, sticky stuff. Seeing that molasses caused me to picture mules going around and around as they provided the horsepower to crush stalks of sugar cane that became dark sorghum. That was energy in the bodies of plowing and planting farm folk I knew in rural South Carolina in the 1950's.

I pictured my thin grandmother – I called her Ma – watching as I used my fourth made-from-scratch biscuit to sop us the last rivulet of golden molasses from one of Ma's chipped, white breakfast plates. I had already eaten sausage, eggs and grits with red-eye gravy.

"Have some more," said Ma, who never worked at a public job. "It'll be a long time before noon."

"I better not," I replied, patting my nine-year-old, fairly good-sized stomach and grinning as I quipped, "The only thing better'n lasses is mo 'lasses."

My grandfather, I called him Pa, smiled and said, "We better get going."

My parents worked in textile mills and let me stay at my grandparent's house on occasions such as corn planting day. Pa was ready to "follow a mule all day" if I helped fill his plows with fertilizer and corn seed. He wore his faded, blue overalls, and I could see the bulge in his buttoned, center-chest overalls pocket where he kept his billfold. Pa usually carried several hundred dollars in his billfold, and Ma worried about that.

"Somebody's liable to knock him in the head," she'd say to me in Pa's presence, and I'd look to see his reaction. Pa was a man of few words, and I never saw him blow up, but when he was irritated, especially with Ma's worrying, I could see his jaw muscles tighten.

Down at the little Pentecostal church we attended, I'd heard a Bible verse that said something about a fellow who had no rule over his own spirit, being like a city that is broken down without walls. Pa wasn't  like that. I figured he was one of those rare men who could rule his own spirit, even though my Uncle Fred said that Pa used to whip him and my father so hard that Ma would be crying and begging Pa to stop. But Pa was different by the time I came along. I never saw the walls of his city broken down.

When I was very young staying with my grandparents one late summer afternoon about milking time, I heard faint, intermittent words wafting on a breeze as Ma and I stood in her kitchen. The words filtered through a raggedy back porch screen door as they floated from the direction of the barn. "What's that?" I asked Ma. "That's Pa," she said. "He's praying."

Immediately I pictured Pa on his knees in the hallway of our barn, and I recalled hearing the older men of our church praying together in an upstairs room above our church sanctuary. The men always prayed loud, and all prayed at the same time. The sounds I heard on the breeze had the same tone of the prayers I heard coming from the room where the older men prayed. I remember nothing of Pa's words, but a warm feeling came over me when Ma said, "That's Pa. He's praying."

As Pa and I prepared to head for the field and our day's work, Ma said something such as, "Now Carl, you don't overdo it. I'll be getting some ice water out to you in a little while."

We passed a corn crib where a black snake usually stayed, and brought Pete, Pa's dark bay mule to drink before harnessing the tall, long eared creature and attaching the trace chains to the distributor plow used to dispense fertilizer. I soon watched Pa, a short man of then 57 years, plow row after row, following in the footsteps of his father.

23

In my mind I can still see Pa plowing, still hear the sound of his prayer-voice floating on a breeze and still hear Ma saying, "That's Pa. He's praying."

The Scriptures tell us, *"Hear my prayer, O Lord, give ear to my supplications: in thy faithfulness answer me, and in thy righteousness"* (Psalm 143:1).

—*Steve Crain*

CHAPTER 5
Heavenly Visitors

I know that angels are posted around us, but have never actually saw them. Well maybe? A few years ago my brother had the idea for he and his wife, my sister and her husband, and Ricky, my husband and I to get away for the weekend together instead of buying Christmas presents for each other. We would go to Boyd Mountain Log Cabins and all share a cabin. We usually spent most of our time hanging out in the cabin together.

Wanda, my brother's wife, would make her potato soup and chicken noodle soup for supper on Friday night and on Saturday morning we cooked breakfast. The first year after Ricky passed was hard for us. We missed him so much. He was always the first one up in the mornings and always made coffee and read his Bible before the rest of us got up. When I woke up he would bring me a cup of coffee. On Saturday morning this first year after Ricky had passed, I got up to the smell of coffee brewing. I thought my brother had gotten up and made coffee, even though I knew he didn't drink it. I didn't think much about it until breakfast when he asked me what time I got up and made coffee. I said I didn't, that I thought he did. Renee and Eric, my sister and her husband, joined in and said they smelled it too.

None of us made coffee that morning, yet we all smelled coffee brewing. The scent filled the cabin. Can I explain it? No. But I know God used it to comfort us bringing back special memories of Ricky.

One year my grandson, Caden, was staying with me and he went with my brother, sister and family to the same Boyd Mountain Cabins.

On the way back home, we stopped in Hendersonville, North Carolina, with my sister, Renee and her husband, Eric. We were walking out of the Mast General Store and out of the corner of my eye I noticed a man looking at us and smiling. He walked up and started talking to us. There was something special about this man. He was really friendly and had a sweet smile. He knelt down to Caden's level and started talking to him about the planets that were visible in the sky and pointing them out to him.

Caden loved it! Ricky and I always loved to watch the stars and planets at this time of year. When he had finished his story, he said good-bye and started to walk away. I told Renee we should have gotten a picture with Caden and him.

When I turned to ask him if he would mind, he was nowhere to be seen. He was there one second and had disappeared the next. Right at that minute, I realized how much he looked like Ricky at a younger age when we first met. I told Renee what I was thinking and she agreed. I'm really beginning to believe that even though our loved ones are gone, they're never really far away.

My son, Luke loved to play on Daddy and Mama's front porch when he was a baby. He would look in the window at Daddy and play with him through the glass. He would look in the window and knock. Daddy would come to the window laughing and say, "Hey Smiley!" They would just giggle.

Luke was 16 months old when Daddy and Mama passed. One night after we had put Luke to bed we heard him laughing and talking. I went into his room and asked, "Luke, who are you talking to?" He said, "That man over there," and pointed to the corner of the room. Luke was looking at him and smiling. I said, "What man, Luke?" and he said, "That man calls me Smiley." This went on for a few nights afterwards.

I can't explain what was happening, because I don't think people come back as angels. I believe angels are separate beings, but we just might still be entertaining an angel unaware.

God's Word tells us, *"Take heed that ye despise not one of these little ones; for I say unto you, That in heaven their angels do always behold the face of my Father which is in heaven"* (Matthew 18:10).

—*Tammy Pridmore*

CHAPTER 6
A Day at the Lake

One of our favorite pastimes on long, hot summer weekends was boating on the lake. My husband, Noah, and I were young and had two daughters that loved to play in the water as much as we did. We would pack up the truck and boat and head out to the lake every chance we got. A picnic lunch, snacks and usually a friend or two was always welcome. Water skiing and swimming, the perfect way to spend a summer weekend. Most times we camped out overnight.

I remember one weekend just our family went out on the boat. We rode all across the lake admiring the beauty of Lake Keowee with the mountains as backdrop to the water. It was a piece of heaven and so relaxing, when suddenly our boat motor made a terrible sound and immediately cut off. Noah worked and worked on it and finally got it cranked back long enough to get to the shore at our camp site. He spent the next two or three hours trying to get it to run. Finally, just as easily as it quit running, he got it fixed and we were off to try it again.

We had not gotten far out in the lake when we saw another couple with two small children on their boat that was not running either. Noah, being the "boat repairman," had to go over and see if he could fix their boat too.

They were driving a nice, shiny inboard boat with a brand-new engine. We had a ten or fifteen-year-old tri-hull Chaparral with a 75-horsepowered Evinrude outboard motor, that had definitely seen its better days. There is nothing worse than a boat new or old that strands you on the lake as we all knew.

After much checking and re-checking everything on the boat, Noah and the guy decided it was hopeless. Neither one knew anything about boat engines, especially new ones. By this time all the children, theirs and ours, were tired and fussy and just wanted to get to the camping sites and play. Much time had passed with no activity for them and of course they were hot and hungry.

Noah told the man that he would just hook to their boat and pull them to shore where he could load his boat on the trailer and get it checked out. The man was really put out because this was their first time taking his boat out and it had broken down.

He finally got it to shore and immediately tried to pay Noah for putting so much time trying to help them. Noah refused and said, "I didn't do much helping, but I wanted to try. I wouldn't want to be stuck out in the lake after dark. I'm glad I could at least get you to shore."

They abandoned their camping idea and the man went and got his truck and they loaded the boat on the trailer and pulled out of the parking lot towards home. In just a few minutes, we see them turning around and coming back towards us. We wondered what was wrong and went to check.

The man said, "We feel bad about you taking all your family time helping us and if you won't take any money, let me give you this just in case." He handed Noah a business card, which he stuck in his pocket.

When we returned home, Noah pulled the card out and this is what it read, Steven J. Merck, Attorney at Law, his address in Georgia, and his phone number with a handwritten note on the back.

The note read, I am an attorney for the State of Georgia, but I am licensed in North Carolina and South Carolina too. If you ever need an attorney for *anything*, I am available free of charge, no matter what the time or need, just call me!

You just never know when you help someone. Not that it matters, but what does matter is our willingness to help. It turns out we never needed his services, but it sure was a nice gesture on his part and a wonderful way to show his thanks.

God's Word says, *"Be not forgetful to entertain strangers: for thereby some have entertained angels unawares"* (Hebrews 13:2).

—*Kathy Lark*

CHAPTER 7
God's Blueprint

When we can't see a way through the trials of life, don't worry, God has a plan. From my youth until now, 55 years old, He has always guided me in the path I was to walk. He is always on time, even though it may not have been on my time. His timing is perfect.

Five years old: I woke up one morning with extreme pain in my stomach. My mama and Sheila, my aunt, rushed me to the hospital. My appendix had ruptured. My daddy was on a fishing trip with my Uncle Noah and my family had to find them on the lake, which was near impossible. They finally made it home and rushed to the hospital. I don't remember anything else until after surgery. My daddy said I almost died that day. A few days later I developed an infection and had to go back for a second surgery. A piece of gauze was left inside my abdomen causing an infection.

Eleven years old: I was playing at my Grandma Greene's house with Eddie. We loved playing outside climbing trees. We were told not to go into the woods while my parents were gone, we were supposed to stay in the yard and play. The temptation was so great we just had to go in those woods. Well, we did and was having a grand ole' time until I stepped on a tree limb and face planted on a broken

Pepsi bottle. When I stood up my leg bent forward and I fell back on the ground. A big chunk of flesh fell out of my pants leg. The neighbor carried me inside until the ambulance came and took me, once again, to the hospital. I was brave until I heard my mama and daddy's voice. Then I started to cry. The diagnosis again wasn't good; I could lose the use of my leg. For a full eight weeks I wore a cast. I had to learn to walk again. It was a long recovery, but family helped me through.

Eighteen years old: I wasn't known for making the best decisions so after I graduated high school, I married the wrong guy, divorced and remarried, again another wrong guy. The third time I got it right; I met and married again. God sent Eric. I married my soulmate in 2000. We have two children, a son Zachary and a daughter, Erica.

Then my world came crashing down. In April of 2001 my mama and daddy were murdered. They were beaten to death with a baseball bat by a crazed killer. I found out while I was at work when Eric came and told me. I was three months pregnant at the time. We had to go into hiding. He was on the loose and was still a danger to my family. After a few harrowing days, he was finally caught, convicted and placed on death row where he was for 24 years. He was executed by firing squad on March 7, 2025.

I was told I couldn't have children after my appendix ruptured. Then I went to the doctor with what I thought was a stomach bug. It was not a bug, but a baby.

When I had Zachary, I was so scared knowing I would have to deliver without my mama or daddy there. Eric was with me the whole time and we brought home our baby boy. Three days later Zachary had some breathing issues and had to return to the hospital. Later he developed seizures, due to high fever. These continued for several months every time he had a fever. After prayer, God healed him.

We got pregnant a second time and had a baby girl, Erica. Our children are precious gifts and God gave them to us. It was all in His plan.

There's nothing like a car wreck to get your attention. We were t-boned by a lady who was running from the police. She hit us so hard we were trapped in the car for a while. A couple of inches over and we would not have survived. Again it was all in God's plan for us.

So I leave with you words of wisdom learned throughout my life. You can't outrun God, and you can't out plan God. Whatever you face, no matter how bad it seems at the time, you can make it through it. God always leads us as we go through many trials and hardships, so turn your life over to Him and trust God's bigger plan!

The Bible reminds us, "*And we know, all things work together for good to them that love God, to them who are the called according to his purpose*" (Romans 8:28).

—Renee Smith

CHAPTER 8
Miracles Still Happen

I have been a Christian for a long time. Not just a Christian in name only, but I am forgiven, shown mercy and grace and paid for by His blood. I believe in healing and I believe every word that is written in the Bible. I most definitely believe in miracles, because I received one in May of 2015. God can do anything He chooses. It's not what doctors say, it's not what science says, it's what the God of the universe decrees.

In February of 2011, my mama passed away and a short six weeks later, in April of the same year, my husband, Noah, my soulmate, yes, I had a soulmate, they do exist, was hit and killed on the side of the road by a driver high on drugs. My family and I received many answers to prayers (miracles) during these terrible days, but through it all, we could feel the presence of God. We received miracles that only God could give. Little did we know that more hard times were just around the corner.

God more than proved Himself to me over and over again. So when my health problems began, I knew God would once again come through for me. For several years I had problems with my liver. I was eventually diagnosed with a fatty liver or NASH (non-alcoholic steatohepatitis).

Before you think the worse, I didn't drink alcohol, use drugs or even smoke. I thought I was doing all the right things to stay healthy.

All the information we could gather about NASH was scary and most of it were things we don't like to think about. The doctors said NASH sometimes progresses slowly and in my case it did, fifteen long years. This disease could eventually cause cirrhosis and then liver cancer and if left untreated it ultimately caused a slow death. Slowly but surely all these horrors begin to come to pass. These were the doctor's words, but not God's.

When I received the NASH diagnosis, my doctor referred me to a liver specialist at MUSC (Medical University of South Carolina). This referral that lasted for years, made it so much easier when the liver cancer was found because I was already an established patient at MUSC. I was immediately sent to Charleston to get numerous tests, MRIs, CT scans, blood work, body scans and evaluations. All of these to determine if I would be a candidate for a liver transplant. Finally after several months, on my sixtieth birthday, and many pokes and sticks later, I was placed on the UNOS (United Network for Organ Sharing) liver transplant list.

I knew other people who had the same diagnosis as me, but I also knew God was working in my life because I had no pain as most people do at this stage. As strange as it may seem, the psychiatric testing was one of the hardest parts of the testing to undergo. Many people, some in my family included, never got past this stage. Not only physically but mentally, cirrhosis is a beast to deal with. The mental evaluation is a long three or four-hour test that asks hundreds of questions that are repetitive. After taking a half-day to complete, my diagnosis was really the kicker. I was fat! That's it! I was too fat and needed to lose weight. They could have took one look at me and determined that. At least I had no mental problems. (I don't know after all these tests.) The last question the psychiatrist asked was the most significant to me. She asked if since the news of my cancer and transplant report, did I feel like my faith in God was shaken? She definitely didn't know me! I calmly replied God has brought me too far to give up on Him now. I knew God had me and my situation in His hands. Nothing they said or did could change my faith in God.

One morning while at MUSC, I had a procedure on the schedule called, chemoembolization or transarterial/ TACE. The procedure wasn't a hard one, just a little scary. Of course I was nervous and it was showing. It was to shrink the liver cancer to keep it from spreading until I was transplanted. I was awake the whole time and could see what they were doing. When I looked around I saw several young doctors and nurses. Young enough for me to be their grandmother. The lead doctor asked me if I liked music. I said sure, I like some older country music and gospel. I was expecting him to put me some headphones on, but instead the entire room of doctors and nurses began to sing. Their singing was absolutely beautiful. My fear was forgotten as time flew by.

This is just one example of the type of hospital MUSC is. They are on the cutting edge of medicine and do the almost impossible every day. Some of the top doctors in the country come from MUSC and it shows. They are caring and genuinely get to know their patients. Now almost ten years later, I still ask my transplant coordinator questions. She never ignores me and always calls back within a day or two with the answer. My doctor is the same. I don't think I would be here today had it not been for my dedicated transplant team.

believe
IN
miracles

I was officially placed on the transplant list in April 2015 and one week later on a Friday afternoon, I received my first call that a liver was available. I had heard stories of people who had to wait months and even years for a liver and I got the call in a week! God was at work. We made the four-hour trip to MUSC only to be told I was second in line for this liver. The person in line before me had received it, as is often the case in transplants. We went back home to await "THE CALL" which came two weeks later on a Sunday afternoon in May. People asked many times after the first call if I was disappointed that I didn't receive the first liver. My reply was always no because I knew God would chose the liver He wanted for me. I would trust His decision. God was always in control.

I will always be grateful to my donor for her sacrifice. Had it not been for being a perfect match and her willingness to be a donor, I could have been waiting much longer for a liver, maybe years. My prayers still go out to her family.

Finally on May 9, 2015, after a sixteen-hour surgery, my transplant was complete with only a few problems. I stayed in the hospital for twelve days and in a local hotel for nine days making me in Charleston for a total of twenty-one days. Originally I was told I could be there for three months. I have been taken off all medicine but one, after just a few months. In the beginning I was told I could be on as many as fifteen. All of these were miracles sent by God. God is good! All the time!

Now ten years later I go back to MUSC for a yearly checkup and every four months for routine blood work at my local hospital. Everything is going as God planned and I thank Him for it all. Also much appreciation and thanks to my donor, my doctors, and my daughters, who were my caregivers throughout this whole ordeal. Thanks to a special twelve-year-old girl who was my home "nurse," my grand-daughter, Katelyn. I often lovingly call her Nurse Kratchet. She was determined to get me well and force me to drink those horrible chocolate shakes! Many thanks to my pastor at the time, Reverend Raymond Burrows, my church, my family, my friends, and all who prayed for me. Please know, God listens and prayer changes things!

My ongoing prayer is to live for Jesus until He calls my name that final time. He has been and always will be my Rock, my Salvation and my Miracle Worker! The lyrics of the old song goes: *He's still working on me to make me what I ought to be. It took Him just a week to make the moon and the stars, the sun, the earth and Jupiter and Mars. How loving and patient He must be. He's still working on me!*

God says, *"Fear thou not; for I am with thee: be not dismayed; for I am thy God: I will strengthen thee; yea, I will help thee; yea, I will uphold thee with the right hand of my righteousness"* (Isaiah 41:10).　　　　　*—Kathy Lark*

CHAPTER 9

A Touch

Chickens! Who likes chickens anyway? Some people love to feed and nurture these pesky, ornery creatures, but they just don't earn any brownie points from me. A lot of them are downright mean and love to plot against us when we are least expecting it. At least this has been my experience most of my life. Mama had chickens when I was growing up and now my daughter Christi has them. She raised her chicks in an incubator and they really live up to the rumors that surround them. For some unknown reason chickens that are incubated seem to be meaner that any others. Actually the only good things about chickens in general are fried chicken, eggs and of course, this story I'm about to tell you.

It happened one sunny day in the middle of the summer when Christi and I went out to gather eggs from the chicken coop in her backyard. She had eight hens and one horrible, nasty rooster! He was the boss of the yard and took every opportunity to let us know it. He would attack unprovoked every chance he got. Today was no exception. I'm not sure of his breed, all I know was that he was red and mean!

One thing I always loved about the concept of owning chickens was getting to gather the eggs from the coop after the hens were off the nest. Something about finding an egg made me think of treasure hunting, which I loved. The thrill of hunting and finding, I suppose.

How I got on this rant of chickens is neither here nor there in the story, but just a little background as to my whereabouts and thoughts that day.

Now back to the story. On this beautiful afternoon while I was watching Christi gathering eggs and putting them in her basket, out of nowhere I felt an ever so light touch on my left shoulder. This touch was so real, I literally looked around to see who had touched me. No one was there! Not even the rooster who I thought was maybe the culprit. I was too embarrassed to say anything for fear of being thought a little crazy, so I said nothing.

I know all of us at times have had strange, un-explained things occur when we are just going about our business. Maybe the feeling of being watched, or a second of irrational fear for no reason, or having that "gut feeling" that something is wrong. On the other hand we may feel like someone is there protecting us or watching over us even if we can't see them. I believe these feelings may be God's way of showing us that He is present even if we can't see Him. I have learned throughout life to never ignore that "gut feeling." Some may call it hearing God's still small voice in our minds.

So if ever on an ordinary, seemingly uneventful day, you experience a touch, a thought or a feeling of not being alone, don't just dismiss it, you may be entertaining an angel unaware.

Now when I think back, with those little pieces of memory we sometimes have, I realize the touch was real and it was an experience that Jesus had intended just for me. It needs no explanation, only belief. The scripture that inspired this story came immediately to mind. *"And Jesus came and touched them, and said, Arise, and be not afraid"* (Matthew 17:7).

—Kathy Lark

CHAPTER 10
Learning From Pa

The cool summer evening settled on the little mid-1950's farm carved into the landscape of the Blue Ridge community north of Greer in upper state South Carolina. I sat on the big rock used as a step for the little porch fronting my grandparent's white frame house. My bare feet felt free as they rested on sandy soil.

The grandson of a carpenter and a housewife who hadn't given up farming and the old ways, I felt glad they still had two mules and a cow, a few chickens and two beagles.

I was proud that each year they bought a suckling pig, slopped it until it was full grown, and used it for its intended purpose when autumn's chill came to our rolling hills. I was allowed to miss school at Mountain View Elementary on the day the butchering was done. That day had to be "cold enough to kill a hog" or the meat would spoil during processing.

Carl and Lillian Crain, my grandparents, Ma and Pa I called them, rested on the porch near me as evening settled and lightning bugs prepared to sparkle.

Being eight years old, I felt my worries held in check by the presence of Ma and Pa, the cool evening

and the Lord. I learned about Him at Gum Springs Pentecostal Church not many miles away. I learned the Lord says, "The night comes when no man can work."

To some that verse might strike fear, might make them think, "I better get busy. Time is running out." But to an eight-year-old that verse can be comforting and a kind of relief where you can rest from the day's work and not feel guilty.

Pa, a short man who gained a stomach after he threw his last pack of Camel cigarettes down through the cornfield, sat on the porch in a rocker. Ma, as tall as Pa and a lean worrying type, sat nearby. Her thin wire-rimmed glasses blended with the slivers of silver in her once raven black hair.

In the dimness of the evening, I saw a figure coming from beyond our red dirt driveway that circled a huge oak tree. It was Brother Grady.

Brother Grady had never visited Pa's house, as I remembered, but here he came about dusk, and he only wore long trousers with no shirt or shoes. His gold wire-rimmed glasses sat propped on his pointed nose, and his sandy colored, thinning hair stood close-cropped in crew-cut style.

Brother Grady attended our church and it struck me as he approached that his lack of a shirt seemed a little out of place. I thought he should have had something covering his nakedness. His fair-skinned belly bulged and gray hairs briar-patched from his chest.

Pa moved to one side of the step and Brother Grady sat beside him. I moved to Pa's chair and listened as the men talked. At one point Brother Grady looked at Pa and said with a grin, "I feel like I've backslid. My back is getting so slick."

Maybe Brother Grady was feeling a little self-conscious about his lack of clothes, but I thought his joking about back sliding was a little strange, us being Pentecostals and all. I felt embarrassed for Ma. She remained silent, but I saw her shift her position a little.

Pretty soon, the night was coming on. Brother Grady finally said he had to "go to the house" and we watched as his white back disappeared beyond the barn as the night absorbed his figure.

Pa just grinned and said nothing. He was always a man of few words. That's why the little he said always meant a lot to me.

We hated to leave the cool porch, but the mosquitoes were bothering us some. Ma opened the screen door and waited for us to enter the dimly lit front room. She said, "That was sort of strange – Grady coming over here with no shirt and saying that about backsliding."

Pa just smiled a little bit and said nothing.

A boy can learn a lot from his grandfather. Sometimes I wish I'd learned his ways a little better.

The Word tells us, *"My son, hear the instruction of thy father, and forsake not the law of thy mother"* (Proverbs 1:8).

— *Steve Crain*

CHAPTER 11

My Little Children

I lived with my maternal grandparents, Mr. James S. Coster and Mrs. Lettie Mae Stewart Coster at the crossing of Groce Meadow Road and Fews Bridge Road. We lived south of Mountain View Elementary School in rural Greenville County, South Carolina.

My mother was Betty Jean Coster who lived in Greenville, South Carolina, so she could ride the trolley to work. She visited us often and one of my favorite memories was her record player. She would let me play all the records I wanted. My favorite song was "Mack the Knife" and hers was "Still." I didn't know who my father was until I was 37 years old. His name was Paul V. Few. Unbeknownst to me, I had two half-sisters, two half-brothers and a stepmother, Virginia Few.

My dad and I got to know each other and as we got closer we found out we had many things in common. We had collected the same collectibles and liked the same foods. I even learned that he come to my sports games as I played.

I attended Gum Springs Pentecostal Church at first, then we moved to Faith Temple Church. I got different rides to church on Sundays. Grady Atkins, who had a Cadillac, let me sit near the door. Eva and Connie Bishop had a 1959

Ford. When I rode with the Ray Hill family I sat where there was room.

When I was eleven years old in 1963 I attended a Jim and Tammy Baker revival at Faith Temple in Taylors, South Carolina, where James "Jimmy" Thompson was the pastor. At regular church when the offering plate came by, I only had a dime, most time, to put in. I was not a big tither.

My pastor came by many times and talked to my grandfather, who was affected by a stroke. I would sneak and listen to see if my grandpa would say "yes," because Pastor Thompson would never leave until he asked, "Mr. Coster, would you like to accept the LORD Jesus as your savior?" Many times my grandfather would say, "Not today." Pastor Thompson would say, "Okay, can I pray before I leave?" and Grandpa would say, "Yes."

Pastor Thompson came never expecting anything in return, for we didn't have anything to give, but we wanted to. Even so, he never stopped coming, and finally one day, I heard my grandfather say "Yes." I cried from my hiding place.

Pastor Thompson was a warrior for the Lord! He had a beautiful wife, Mrs. Joanne Thompson. She was my Bible school teacher, which was a treat within itself. We once made pigs from Clorox bottles. I never forgot about making these pigs with her. She had the patience of Job. She showed me what a Christian was supposed to be. The love of my young life was *Wonder Woman*, but since she was only on TV, Mrs. Thompson was my real *wonder woman.*

I played sports at Blue Ridge High School and had an offer to play for Clemson's Coach Howard, but enlisted in the Army instead where I became a drill sergeant. I then took a job as a South Carolina Highway Patrolman. I married Jan M. Powell and had three children, Melissa, Mathew and John.

At this time I was doing what I wanted. My wife took our children to church and I stayed in bed because I worked late. I was working, on the side, at a place called Dillion's standing at the door keeping bad people from entering the building. As I stood by the dance floor an angel of God spoke to me and said, "I want you to take a good look and tell me if these people are really happy. This is not your place! Your place is at home with your wife and children."

I walked out, got in my truck, and drove home. I promised God I would go to church the next Sunday if He would keep me.

The thing that broke me was hearing my little girl was at church, crying, and after they got her calmed down, she said, "I do not want my daddy to go to hell!"

At church the alter call came and I jumped to my feet, stepping on people's toes as I went. I'm thankful to God that I had good people to lead me. I still have a picture of me and some of these people. I now can look back with fond memories in my old age.

I remember Pastor Jimmy Thompson would always shake my little hand with his big hand and say, "David, you look out for Grandma and Grandpa," and I would say, "Okay!" I think he was the only man who ever shook my hand when I was a child!

God's Word reminds us, *"Only take heed to thyself, and keep thy soul diligently, lest thou forget the things which thine eyes have seen, and lest they depart from thy heart all the days of thy life: but teach them thy sons, and thy sons' sons"* (Deuteronomy 4:9).

—*David Coster*

CHAPTER 12
The Shoes

This story is written about an incident that was told to me by my grandson. It's his account of what happened one night while on patrol.

My story begins when I decided that I wanted to become a police officer. Not at the age of 21 or 25, but four years old. I know every kid at one time wants to be a policeman and I was no exception. I guess we are in awe of the lights, sirens, guns and fast cars. Even grown I am still in awe sometimes. My uncle is a policeman and I always wanted to do the "police" work I'd see him do.

Fast forward about fifteen years and here I am, now a police officer. I work both early and late hours, and meet people from every walk of life, including my wife. Yeah, who would have thought I would meet the love of my life on my job. God works in mysterious ways. There is never a night or day that we don't experience the best and the worst of humanity. We hear every made-up and wild story known to man as well as many sad and heartbreaking true stories. Our lives go from high to low in a 24-hour period. One of the most memorable events that really sticks with me was on a chilly, dark night in the downtown area where I worked at the time. I was a new officer on the force and ready to save the world. I received a call on the radio to go to a certain address.

I immediately recognized the address. It was a guy that I often had to visit due to questionable behavior and activities. Often times I think he just wanted some attention, good or bad. Tonight was no different. Someone had called the police on him for doing whatever he chose to do that particular night.

Hoping for a peaceful resolution and getting things settled down, without an arrest, I spent a few minutes talking to him and was able to get him on his way. As he walked off down the street, I noticed he had an odd way about his walk. I called him back to me. When I looked down, I saw that he was only wearing socks. Curiosity compelled me ask him where his shoes were. He responded that he didn't know, that he had lost them somewhere. He then turned to walk off. Again I called him back and told him to wait a minute. I went to the trunk of my patrol car and took out my tennis shoes and handed them to him. He looked at me as if to say are you kidding me? He was so surprised and a little excited. He sat down on the curb and put them on his feet. I'm not even sure they fit him. Close enough for him though. You would have thought that I had given him a million dollars he was so happy.

I've learned that people will forget what you said, people will often forget what you did, but people will never forget how you made them feel. I knew I had made an impression on his life that day.

I haven't seen or heard from him lately, which is good news, but I'm sure he's still wearing those shoes. The last time I saw him he was walking away with two "new" shoes on his feet and a spring in his step.

You just never know when someone just needs a hand up. He did and I was there to help. God places us in positions to work for Him. Our work will be blessed if we follow what God plans for us. I try to treat people right and help all I can. Some days I may have to be the bad guy, but such is the life of a police officer!

The Bible tells us that, *"Blessed are the peace-makers: for they shall be called the children of God"* (Matthew 5:9).

—Kathy Lark

CHAPTER 13
Angel by Night

This is a story of an event that took place many years ago in the Dark Corner area of the mountains just inside the South Carolina line. The following is an account told by my late husband, Noah Lark, in his own words.

I had a fun December night, hanging out with old friends. We were having a blast playing records and talking. Just reminiscing about some of the good times we had together through our high school years. That night the clock was ticking and time was slipping away as it often did in my youthful days.

I remember glancing out the window several times that night and seeing snow begin to fall, lightly at first, but gradually getting heavier and heavier.

On my last peek through the window, I realized that if I wanted to make it home, I had better be on my way. My friends assured me that the roads were covered by this hour and I had too many miles to go to even consider making it home. Being hard-headed and strong willed I was determined to go. I knew my dad would be up waiting for me worrying as usual. I wasn't afraid, I loved the slipping and sliding that was sure to happen when I got my car on the road. Boy did things turn out different than expected!

I went out into the night and got into the car. As I looked out across the yard, I could see only the faint outlines of the road, and the long driveway that stretched before me was completely covered by the ever-increasing snowfall. It never took long for snow to accumulate here in the mountains.

Traveling in these places was hard traveling on clear nights, not to mention roads covered with snow. Needless to say, I didn't get very far fast.

By this time the temperature had fallen well below freezing and driving was only getting harder. Why had I ever thought this would be fun? After driving about an hour that seemed like forever, my car begin to sputter and then out of the blue stalled, leaving me stranded. I was on a road with no houses and only a lightweight jacket for protection from the freezing wind that had now begun to blow.

I thought as I sat alone in the car that if I wanted to keep from freezing to death, I had better get out and walk to try to find help, or if nothing else, start moving to keep warm. So I got out and began to walk. I made good time at first, but moved slower and slower with each step I took. The more I walked the colder I got. The wind made my eyes fill with tears that slipped down my face and actually froze before I could wipe them away with the sleeve of my jacket. My vision blurred and I could feel my mind slowly shutting down. I was trying my best to keep my head clear and continue moving. After considering stopping to take a short rest, a thought came from within as a still small voice encouraged me to keep going. Without really knowing why, I listened to the voice. I kept on walking. After what felt like hours, the headlights of an oncoming car in the distance moved toward me. With all the strength I could muster, I waved my arms for the car to stop. It was coming closer to me, but when it reached the place where I stood, it passed by without even slowing down.

The thought of just being left on the side of the road was almost more than I could bear. As my anger subsided, I realized the reason the car had passed. It would be dangerous for someone to stop and pick up a total stranger on the side of the road in the dark.

When these thoughts filtered through my mind, I heard a noise behind me. It was car lights and I could hear a motor running! This time I waved more frantically and the car began slowing down.

I was so thankful at that moment. The driver opened the door and I literally fell inside. He told me he had passed my car a mile or so back and knew I was in danger. He just didn't know how right he was!

I only remember a few pieces of our conversation, but vividly recall asking him his name. After receiving no answer the first time, I asked again, but still no answer, so I let it drop.

After warming up a little, I tried to start another conversation by asking him where he worked. He said he was a mill worker on his way home from his shift. He barely got the answer out of his mouth, and we were pulling onto the driveway that led to my friend's house.

Now when thinking back, I realize it was only a short time we were in the car. It had taken me over an hour before to go the same distance. Also noticing he wasn't dressed like a mill worker or a person who had just left work. My most vivid memory of that night was the color of his hair and his clothes. Both was almost a brilliant white.

The porch light came on to my friend's house. They all came out on the porch just as the car pulled to a stop, not because they had heard anything, but because they were going to get firewood. I jumped out to explain to them what had happened to me.

When the car door shut and I had taken a few steps toward the house, I realized I had forgotten to thank my mysterious rescuer. When I turned to tell him, the driveway was empty! There was no car, no tire tracks, only the same snow-covered yard I had left an hour or so before.

My friends told me they never heard a car, nor did they see who brought me back. Sometimes I pause and ponder what really took place that night. I wasn't dreaming. Can I explain for sure what happened? No! I firmly believe then and still years later that God sent His angel that night to watch over me.

I have never to this day seen this man or his car again. But I know in my heart that I will see Him again; not on a long snow-covered road in the foothills of the Carolina mountains, but in heaven on the streets of gold. I say again, "Thank You Jesus for sending my angel that night!"

God promises us, *"The angel of the Lord encampeth round about them that fear him, and delivereth them"* (Psalm 34:7)

—*Kathy Lark*

CHAPTER 14
Messenger From Heaven

We never know who we will meet nor what a day may bring that could change our lives forever. Certainly we can't see around corners and predict the events that happen to us. If we could, we would make a valiant effort to change our course immediately. This is the story of my sister, Lisa and her tragic encounter with a drunk driver.

The events take place in May 1990 in Pelzer, South Carolina, on a stretch of road near the city. It was a quiet night and she was on her way home from my aunt's house. Minding her own business and making her way down the road, she sees, in the distance, the headlights of an oncoming car veering into her lane. With no time to avoid an accident, the cars collide with the sound of crunching metal.

My aunt actually saw the accident and the people there told her that Lisa had died. After the cars stopped and emergency personnel got on the scene, the full story and the real tragedy is revealed. The car that crossed the center line was carrying three adults and one seventeen-year-old. The driver being intoxicated and the seventeen-year-old being thrown from the car and now deceased. My aunt found out later that it wasn't Lisa who had died but the young girl in the other car. My sister doesn't recollect much of what happened that night, but the events afterwards. I remember well.

All the people involved were taken to the emergency room where three were diagnosed with minor injuries, one pronounced dead and one, Lisa, in critical condition. Lisa had multiple head and face lacerations, some brain swelling, chest trauma, a head fracture, two black eyes, and a broken arm. The doctor thought he may have to do a procedure to relieve pressure on her brain. Thank God that didn't happen. She was in an extremely critical state. I thought she would surely die that night.

Day One: We weren't allowed to stay with her because of her being in the emergency room, so I went home that night not knowing if Lisa would live or die. It was probably the longest night of my life. We slept very little because of worrying. We prayed most of the night. We thought this night would never end.

Day Two: The first thing the next morning, my Nanny and I were at the hospital for an update. We found not much had changed and tests were still being done. They were checking for brain damage, broken bones and of course the head trauma was a concern. We were all a nervous wreck as time dragged by. If you've ever waited in a hospital for news about a loved one, you know the feelings we were experiencing.

Around lunchtime my nanny and I went down to the hospital cafeteria to get a little something to eat. Of course the lines were long and the noise was deafening. Just what we needed.

As we were standing in line waiting, I noticed a man behind us kept looking at me, he finally came up to our table and started talking to us. He said, "Don't think I'm crazy, but I have something to tell you. Last night my wife and I were praying and I was sent to tell you that your sister is going to be okay." I didn't know him and had never seen him before. He looked as if he could have been a worker who was doing the construction upgrades on the building. He was in a uniform as if he had just walked off the job and came to eat.

When he started to talk it seemed like all the background noise in the cafeteria became deathly silent. I couldn't hear the hum of voices and the noise of everyday life in the cafeteria any more. He told us things that there was no way he could know anything about. Only God could know the things he told. He assured me again that Lisa was going to be okay. She would have no permanent damage to her brain. She may have minor wounds, but they would heal and she would be fine. He said, "I saw a bright light walking with her, not dark energy, but light. She's going to be okay." All the while he was talking my nanny didn't say a word. She just listened.

After he left I found myself believing every single word he spoke. My worry left and I began to speak healing from that moment on for Lisa. Why I knew he was speaking the truth, I simply don't know. I just did!

Day Three: From that moment, with worry in the past, I knew Lisa would be healed. As each new day came and went, Lisa improved. After four days in ICU she was placed in a regular room. At this point she had not seen her face lacerations. She looked really bad. Above her bed someone had given her mylar balloons with a reflective side on them. She was looking at the balloons and she caught a glimpse of her face. She immediately asked to see her face, so I took her to the mirror to see. She was appalled at her wounds, but I assured her she was going to be fine. They would all heal in time and she would be back to normal. I then told our family about the man and his words to me. I had my nanny as a witness. Nanny had not spoken a word about it to anyone either and when I confronted her, she just shook her head yes.

Day Four: This new day brought more and more improvement. Before we told her about the young girl dying, doctors were concerned Lisa may need counseling. She ended up never needing counseling and she came home mentally okay. Today there are no lasting effects from the accident.

My curiosity got the best of me and I tried to find the mysterious man. I went to another worker who was there doing some work on the hospital and described our miracle man to him. I asked him if he knew him or had seen him. He said he did not know him but he knew that he had just been pulled from another job to work with him that day. He didn't know his name and had never seen him before, nor since. God had sent His messenger to comfort us!

God tells us 365 times in His Word to not worry or fret. I know we all do at times, but God tells us to trust in Him and keep the faith. God is writing each of our stories. He's writing mine, yours and Lisa's. He knows what He is doing. He has a plan, just let God have the pen.

God says in the Bible, *"Be careful for nothing; but in every thing by prayer and supplication with thanksgiving let your requests be made known, unto God. And the peace of God, which passeth all understanding, shall keep your hearts and minds through Christ Jesus"* (Philippians 4:6-7).

—*Joann Coleman*

CHAPTER 15
Signs and Wonders

Sometimes I have, what I like to call, God moments. Such a moment came one day when I was working on my computer.

My husband, Chris and I were in Charleston, South Carolina. Chris was in a class for his work. I'm working on my computer trying to earn CEU's for my credentials. All is quiet.

It doesn't seem like I get much alone time between work, life and kids...well... much like everyone else, just "busy." I finally had that quiet moment. It had been a few stressful weeks. We had just lost two young kids in our community, which brought me back in time eight years prior. I had lost a friend of 34 years. It just quickly makes you realize behind every smile; there's a battle someone is facing.

The stigma of mental health in America is hard for me to understand. I am all for counselors. There are individuals who really need medicine and some counselors that will really work on helping them to overcome their problems. We must do what we have to do to get these people the help they need. But no, instead, too many individuals are afraid of what others will think. The people in a leadership position speak of anxiety and depression, yet NEVER walked a day in another person's shoes. I don't understand it myself. I've never walked in those shoes. So I'll be the first to say, I'm not the expert. I'll keep my opinions to myself. If you need help call me and I will do everything I can to get you the help you need. So no wonder there is "shame" around getting help when all these unneeded, unwanted, and simply un-warranted opinions are offered. But all the while, these kids are still suffering.

So, as I am sitting on the bed working on the CEU's and living this heaviness, suddenly I hear a flapping sound at the hotel window. I look over and see a bird just flapping around and hitting the window pane with its beak and wings. This went on for over a minute so I snap a picture. After a while it finally stops and just sits still on the window ledge and looks at me. I walk over to the window and snap another picture. When getting a closer look, I see the bird has the brightest blue tail feathers.

Then it hits me, God is always there giving us hope, just waiting in the background. Then sometimes it takes just a simple event, a bird constantly tapping on a window, to grab our attention. I tell my daughter, Harlee, at times He doesn't just give us a sign, he gives us a billboard!

Although you may be sitting in a place that you feel there's no hope and no one can understand what you are going through, you're lost and don't know which way to turn, rest assured, if you look up and lift up your head your redemption is on the way.

All my life I have believed and served a God who is ever present in my times of need. We serve a God that is always on time. He is never late and always has the answers we are needing. Just when we think all hope is lost and we're about to give in or give up, God shows up.

God is our hope. He has a master plan for our lives. There is change and a new beginning headed your way! Remember these words from His Word: *"And when these things begin to come to pass, then look up, and lift up your heads; for your redemption draweth nigh"* (Luke 21:28).

—*Andrea Rosier*

CHAPTER 16
Angel in the River

In 2002 I went on a medical mission trip to Africa that lasted a little over a month. We were in Zimbabwe, Zambia and Johannesburg. Victoria Falls is on their borders. It was here we had our fun day: a time to rest and reflect on all we had done and seen while there.

We decided to go on a white-water rafting trip on the Zambezi River, which is rated the highest level of rafting. There were waterfalls that we were told to avoid so we had to carry our rafts around them carefully crossing over black, hot, sharp rocks. We watched the experts as they would go over the falls. They were along to help in case one of us fell out of the raft and couldn't get back in. They would hold onto us until we could get to a place where we could actually get in our raft each time. These rapids were the roughest I had ever seen.

As we were attempting to maneuver our raft, which was holding seven people, we hit a wave that tipped the raft up causing the guy in front of me to hit me with his arm and flipping me out of the raft, right into the Zambezi. It happened so fast! It was freezing cold even with a wet suit and a life jacket!

I opened my eyes under crystal clear water and I could see those big black rocks as I sped past them! I prayed God would keep me from getting stuck, because when that happens it is almost impossible to get loose because of the strong, raging current.

Right in front of me a man appeared, whether a person or an angel, and said to me, "Sandra, remember what your guide told you to do with your legs." Earlier our guide had told us to hold our knees to our chest and we would rise to the top of the water. So I did. The angel took my right arm, raised it up and my hand immediately touched the rope on the raft. I held on tightly and just went down the river hanging on until the guide lifted me back into the raft with no difficulty. I know that God was taking care of me that day in the water sending His angel to help me.

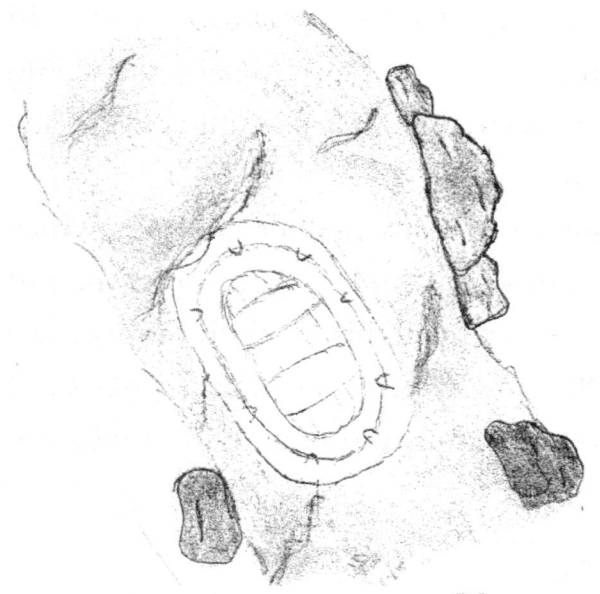

God's Word says, *"For he shall give his angels charge over thee, to keep thee in all thy ways. They shall bear thee up in their hands, lest thou dash thy foot against a stone"*(Psalm 91:11-12).

—*Sandra Greene*

CHAPTER 17
Angel on Duty

My grandson Christian has always been the mischievous and outgoing middle child in the family. He's always the one child that kept us on our toes. An animal lover at heart, he has always had goats, chickens, rabbits, cats or dogs. He also has a special "gift" or insight into things others might not understand. Read on and you will get a glimpse of these unusual abilities.

One of our first experiences was when he was about nine years old. Their family had goats in the pasture in their backyard. One night a pack of wild dogs got into the fence and killed every goat, leaving only two nannies barely alive. They later added more nanny goats with the two, but never bought another Billy goat. When the following story took place almost a year had passed and they still had this same herd.

One night a snowstorm came up during the night. Something apparently woke Christian up from his sleep and a dream he was having. He ran to his parent's bedroom, woke them up and told them what he had been dreaming. He was convinced some of the goats had babies during the storm. He said a baby was going to drown if he didn't go out and save it. His mom told him to just go back to sleep and wait until the storm stopped and then he could go out, check on it. He was having none of that, he was determined to go outside and look for the baby right then. He knew it would be too late and by then it would have drowned or frozen to death. He just would not take no for an answer so she let him put on an oversized coat and go look for the goat.

She watched from the window as he ran through the dark and wondered how he thought there would be a baby goat when there was no Billy goat. He ran straight to the spot the goat was in his dream and disappeared around the corner of the barn. After a short while he came back around the corner and started running for the house. When he got on the front porch, he pulled back the coat for her to see and there was a soaking wet, half-frozen new-born goat in his arms. It was only a few minutes old. A miracle indeed!

There was no way he could have known about this baby. Several other goats had babies that night too, but all were dead except this one. No one knew where this newborn had come from, but somehow Christian had known it was there. He raised it to adulthood until it passed of old age. No Billy goat and a miracle baby? Some things we will never understand or figure out. Maybe we're not supposed to?

Another story that happened when the family went on a fishing trip to Lake Robinson near their home. They left home early one morning to fish from the pier on the lake.

They fished for a while with no luck so they decided to change piers and see if the fishing was better at a new spot.

While they fished, Christi, my daughter, noticed a man in a canoe far out in the water. He was paddling around and just taking his time enjoying the lake like they were. As they moved from pier to pier, Christian was casting his line out farther into the lake repeatedly and in doing so accidentally knocked his new glasses off into the water at the edge of the pier. The man in the canoe was watching at a distance the entire time.

Everyone in the family tried many times to drag the bottom with their poles and hook the glasses out of the water. The water was too deep and murky for them to find them. Greg went back home and got a fishing net to see if it would help to scoop them out. They tried for hours to find the glasses, but nothing worked. They were all tired and just ready to give up.

By this time they had attracted the interest of the man in the canoe and he had paddled closer to see what they were doing. He asked if he could be any help to them. They told him what had happened. He asked if he could try. Of course they let him because they had given up and were more than ready to go home. Here's the miracle of the whole event. The man took the net and pushed it down deep into the water and when he pulled it up, the first time, the glasses were in the net! Nobody could believe it!

They all thanked him for coming to help them and as they began packing up, Christian wanted to say a personal thanks to the man himself for getting his glasses. The man had already left to load his canoe to go home. Christian ran up the short hill beside the lake to thank him, but he was nowhere to be found! There had been no time for the man to load his canoe and leave. Yet he had completely disappeared.

The Bible says to be careful to entertain, whereby some have entertained angels unaware. Who was this man? Where did he come from? More importantly where did he go so quickly? They never found out, but maybe, just maybe, Christian had just met his guardian angel face to face.

Christian is a grown man now and is a police officer. This was always his dream as a child. I believe his angel is still watching over his life protecting him. One thing I know for certain, this angel has his hands full!

The Bible promises, *"For he shall give his angels charge over thee, to keep thee in all thy ways"* (Psalm 91:11).

—Kathy Lark

CHAPTER 18

But God...

I remember loving God from a very young age. Even while playing I remember feeling His presence with me. My love for Jesus has always been with me.

I was very shy as a child. It wasn't until after being saved that I overcame my shyness with God's help. If my testimony had a name it would be, "But God...."

God has always been good to me. He healed me from pneumonia when I was a newborn. I was dying, and as a last resort the doctors decided to pack me in ice. I know God showed the doctors what to do. He healed me and He has always been with me since. But God....

God blessed me with a good family life and with a loving home to grow up in. Even though Daddy and Mama didn't go to church regularly, they loved God. I believe that still. Daddy would read the Bible and pray with me before I would go to bed. Our house was always filled with music, whether it was Daddy singing or music playing on the radio. Daddy and Mama taught us by example how to love family, how to be there for family, and how to sacrifice for the good of the family. But God....

God put people in my life who were influential in teaching me how to live life for God. I will mention some of them, but I am sure in doing so I will probably leave some out. Beginning with my Grandma and Grandpa Lark, Grandma and Grandpa Greene, Noah and Kathy Lark, Sheila Lark Styles, Raymond and Doris Lark, Dennis Greene (after he was saved), Jerry and Thelma Blackstock, Dave and Pam McElrath, Bud Walls, Ricky Pridmore, Mary Hannah, Pastors Frank and Judy Jones, and so on. After my brother Darrell (David) was saved God used him to teach me to live for God. He married Wanda Stokes and God used her and Waldo (Walter) and Jean, her parents, as well. But God....

There was a time when we did go to church as a family. We went to Faith Temple. Jimmy and JoAnne Thompson were used mightily by God to minister to my family. Their influence still lasts today. God brought me the best friend and husband I could ever have – Ricky Pridmore.

We met at Faith Temple. Walter Stokes introduced us. But God….

God has blessed my family with many healing experiences. He healed me of migraines and lymphoma, my daddy of cancer, my sister, Renee when her appendix ruptured when she was a small child. He wooed Daddy and Mama back to Him. At the hardest times of my life God has shown up in a big way. When I have a hard time dealing with many of life's problems, He has never left me. He reminds me He is still here when I think about what happened to Daddy and Mama, my Uncle Noah and Ricky not being here. Even when my children made bad choices, He has always been faithful. He fights my battles. He is truly my everything! But God….

God's Word says, "*For you created my inmost being; you knit me together in my mother's womb. I praise you because I am fearfully and wonderfully made; your works are wonderful, I know that full well. My frame was not hidden from you when I was made in the secret place, when I was woven together in the depths* of the earth. Your eyes saw my unformed body; all the days ordained for me were written in your book before one of them came to be. How precious to me are your thoughts, God! How vast is the sum of them! Were I to count them, they would outnumber the grains of sand — when I awake, I am still with You" (Psalm 139:13-18, NIV).

—*Tammy Pridmore*

CHAPTER 19
When Dreams Come True

We know from accounts in books and interviews many people have dreams and visions. Some feel extremely real, while others are totally off the wall crazy. A few we may remember the next morning but most we never think of again. Dream interpreters believe that dreams come from events that happened during the day that set the dream in motion. Wherever dreams originate, they can be real to the dreamer.

There are twenty-one dreams recorded in the Bible. Only one of them was by a woman. Joseph was known as the dreamer. Jacob dreamed of a ladder. Gideon had a dream about a barley loaf. Pharaoh dreamed about cows and grain. Pilot's wife had a nightmare warning about Jesus. The Magi was warned about Pharaoh wanting to kill Jesus. Thus we see in God's Word dreams are sent as signs to us of things or events that are to come or to warn us of impending danger.

We should never underestimate or second guess the dreams that feel real, nor the ones that we never forget, even years later. I have had a few dreams that I remember each and every detail. I'm sure all of us have. Here is one such dream I had many years ago, fifty-four to be exact, and I have to this day never forgotten the details.

When I was around twenty-four years old my daddy got very sick and no doctor could seem to diagnose his exact problem. He just got worse and worse as months passed. Finally he was placed in the veteran's hospital in Asheville, North Carolina. He stayed there for about two months, all the while never getting any better. They eventually sent him home basically to die with no answers as to why. He passed away two weeks later with an aneurysm that went to his heart causing a massive heart attack.

We had tried everything we knew to get answers, but we never could get anything concrete at all. This left us wondering as to the reason why someone could get sick so quickly and die, leaving us with more questions than answers.

My greatest fear was that my daddy had died and I wasn't sure if he was a Christian when he passed. This bothered me more than words can say. I said many prayers asking God just to give me some kind of assurance that he was saved and in heaven.

Two days before he passed away, I went to visit him and I could tell it wouldn't be long before he left this world. He asked me that night several times to go turn his car around in the driveway. I never knew what this was all about, but to satisfy him, I did as he asked. I turned the car around and came back inside and told him I had turned it around and it was ready to go. Feeling in my heart this was his way of letting me know he was ready to go and leave this world behind. Soon after, he started telling me about a river that he was wading in and exclaiming that the water was so clear that he could see his feet through it. I knew he was describing to me a place that only he could see.

About an hour after this exchange, he slipped into eternity with the heart attack. Just that quick his life on this earth was over. I felt good about the things he was seeing and started to believe he really saw a glimpse of heaven. This was God's way of letting me know he was saved. I still had lingering doubts and prayed for another sign from God to reassure me. That assurance came in a dream a few weeks later.

When he was in the veteran's hospital, we always drove up to see him on Thursdays and Sundays every week. In the dream I was on one of these visits. I saw him in a large hospital room with nine other men. It was similar to an ICU, only bigger. The patients in the room were being monitored twenty-four hours a day with a machine and a nurse at the head of each bed. His bed was on the right side of the room. I walked over to his bed and sat on the side all the while thinking how sick he looked as he lay peering up at me. We had a short conversation and in the middle of us speaking, he sat up beside me. He hadn't been able to sit up alone for several days. As he got up, I suddenly realized he didn't look sick any more. I saw his hands that had gotten so slim from all his weight loss was fuller and healthy looking like they had been before. He still wore his black onyx ring with his initial "R" engraved in it. Saying nothing to him about what I was thinking, we went on with the conversation. Getting close to the end of the visit, he looks at me and his exact words were, "Well, I've got to go be with my girl now." Just remembering he had passed away a few days before, my first thought was that he didn't have a girl to go be with. I said, "You don't have another girl." He replied, "Yes, I do." I woke up and just that quick the dream had ended.

Later that night as I pondered on his parting words, I realized he had just told me he had another girl that none of us knew anything about. I could not wait to ask my mama about it the next morning. Early the next day I went to see my mama and asked her what he could have meant. Shocked knowing that there was no way I could know anything about her miscarriage, she explained that she had lost a baby many years before and they had kept it to themselves and never told anyone about it.

With haste, I told her all about the dream and that I believed the baby that they lost was in fact a little girl. I asked her did she know if the baby was a boy or a girl? She said it had died too early and doctors were unable to determine the sex.

To this day I have never forgotten a single moment of this dream. I firmly believe when I get to heaven, I'll meet the sister I never knew I had.

The Bible says, *"And it shall come to pass in the last days, . . . your young men shall see visions, and your old men shall dream dreams:"* (Acts 2:17).

—Kathy Lark

CHAPTER 20

A Healing Jesus

It was mid-summer in 2024, I went to visit my oldest brother in New Mexico. I had a great time with my family while I was there. My brother never got to attend church with us, but I went every week with one of my nieces. It was on a Sunday that my incident happened.

The last Sunday before I was planning to return home, we went out to eat after Sunday school. When we left, I suddenly realized I couldn't fasten my seat belt when I got in the car, which was really strange. I really didn't think a lot about it, but when I got out of the car to walk into the house, my drink slipped out of my hand and hit the ground. I was not having trouble walking, but I felt funny in my head. Sort of woozy feeling.

Not sure what was happening, I went to my room to change clothes and laid down on my bed. My niece came in to check on me. She was concerned so she had my brother's caretaker check my sugar level and blood pressure. Both were okay.

Since these unusual episodes had happened, we decided I should go to the hospital and be checked out just to be on the safe side. When we arrived at the hospital and they asked me to sign some papers, I couldn't even sign my name. My right hand would not work. All these strange episodes together had my attention.

They immediately sent me for tests and determined I'd had a parallel stroke. Given the situation, I made the choice to go on to Amarillo, Texas, for further testing.

I was in the hospital for three days while they did all the usual procedures for stroke patients. Weakness was my main problem at the time.

It is now the middle of March and I am doing fine. I flew home on August 31 with the assistance of a young man who helped me on the plane in Fort Worth. I had a good flight home.

At home I went through occupational and speech therapy. The neurologist and the heart doctors both said there was no medical reason for me having a stroke that they could find.

Thank God, I have no aftereffects from the stroke. I'm not able to put into words what I want to say some times, but I am getting better, praise God.

I do know there were many people praying for me and I am convinced prayer changes situations and circumstances.

God heard and answered the prayers that people prayed during that time. He is with us through every trial we face. God is good. All the time! His Word says, *"For I will restore health unto thee, and I will heal thee of thy wounds, saith the LORD..."* (Jeremiah 30:17).

—*Doris Via Taylor*

CHAPTER 21

God Moments

I guess you could consider this another one of those, what I liked to say "God moments". Twice today this song came on the radio… *"Can He, Could He, Would He. . ."* by Ernie Haase and Signature Sound.

After hearing the song twice in one day, it made me really start looking at the words.

Can He: If we are honest, there are probably many times in life we all may ask that question. But in Matthew it states, "But *Jesus beheld them and said unto them, "With men this is impossible, but with God all things are possible"* (Matthew 19:26). So, can he? Yes, He can!

Could He: Now, if you've walked through the fire, much like my family has for 23+ years, we already know that answer. *"Look at the birds of the air; they do not sow or reap or store away in barns, and yet your heavenly Father feeds them. Are you not much more valuable than they?"* (Matthew 6:26). So, could He? Yes, He could!

Would He: Many times, throughout the Bible, we are taught that He would. I think of Abraham and Sarah, where many thought they would never have children. Yet, God made a way. Then you read where the lady suffered with a disease for 12 years but knew if she could just touch the hem of His garment, she would be healed. Personally, I know of His healing power. After going to the eye doctor for years, on one visit with the ophthalmologist, he looked at me and said, "Have I ever told you that you had a freckle in your eye?" I said never. He immediately sent me to a retina specialist. Now another God moment ... this retina specialist had recently moved into the area and is one of the only surgeons in the southeast that is qualified to treat the condition that I had. Now, although the doctors like to call it a freckle, on the first visit, the nurse seemed to call it at face value. She proceeds to walk in the exam room and states, "I'll pull up the pictures of the tumor." So, of course, I'm then petrified. The physician completes all his scans and then proceeds to explain I have three things working against me. It's raised, it has orange pigmentation, and it is sitting directly on my optic nerve. If this was anywhere else, he would immediately biopsy it. However, due to where it is located, if he went in to biopsy the area, I would definitely lose the site in that eye. But then he proceeds to look at me and state... "But, if we get to that point, I'm not trying to save your sight... I would be trying to save your life." So, I left the office that day in tears and in a panic not knowing what the future may hold. He wanted me back in to recheck and he did this several times over the next few months. On one of those visits, he said "That doesn't seem possible." So of course, I had to ask what he meant, and he proceeds to say, "Those things do not shrink. But looking at it today, I would think it's smaller than it's ever been." I just smiled and said, "OH YES it could!" For what he didn't know... there had been many prayers going up on my behalf. "*O Lord my God, I cried to you and thou hast healed me*" (Psalm 30:2). So, would he? No doubt in my mind.

Did He: Absolutely yes! In the conclusion to my personal story above... I am honored to say, I sit here just hitting the sixth anniversary of the original diagnosis of the tumor "freckle." It continues to be the same size and shown no growth. I'm not eligible for any trial studies. The physician has said at this point if he tried to send me to one, they would laugh him away since it has been several years with absolutely no changes. The physician even commented that if it was any other ophthalmologist that I had been seeing, he would be convinced that it was a missed diagnosis and there since birth. However, with that doctor he has seen too many cases that are truly legit, and he is convinced that it is not something that he would have just overlooked.

It's been so stable, that several years ago I was released to yearly checks. One of the follow-ups checks with my ophthalmologist, I told him the story... and the fact I knew it was possible for all the many prayers that went up. He looked at me and asked, "Andrea, do you mind if I pray with you?" Of course, I said absolutely not, I do not mind at all! Not many times a doctor will stop an office visit and take the time to pray but I do thank God for the ones that will!!! *". . . but God has surely listened and has heard my prayer"* (Psalm 66:19). So, did He? Absolutely!

If you are sitting there in life, facing a situation where there doesn't seem to be hope, know that if He did it for me, beyond a shadow of a doubt, He can do it for you! Just remember... Yes, He can. Yes, He could. Yes, He would. AND... YES, He did!!!

—Andrea Rosier

CHAPTER 22
Rock Bottom

There was a dark time in my life in 2001 when I felt like my world was turned upside down. Nothing was like I dreamed when I was a young child growing up. Every memory that I had held onto as a child seem to be disappearing the older I got. The simple things got harder and harder.

As the years passed the same sense of change took over me and my children. Our lives as we had known as a young family had gone forever. I know for a fact, one year, one decision, or one bad choice can make a lifetime of difference in this world. The decisions that we make affect others, no matter, how much we may not want to believe it.

I was in a relationship with a man for five years who I thought was my best friend. As time passed we grew closer and felt confident enough that our love would last. I had found someone to be my permanent mate.

Our lives looked so promising that we thought we had it all. A happy home, healthy children and a good start in life. As time passed, my mate became a different person. Little things began to change. Something was in the air and I could feel it. He started to spend less time at home with us and more time going out places. Where? I had no idea. I would beg him to stay home and keep our family together, but nothing worked. This became the pattern every week. I later found out he was cheating. Things got much worse at home and finally when I had enough, I moved out. I took the children and left him behind.

We had been out of the house for about three months when our long nightmare began.

He hit his boiling point and one morning he came to my house and kidnapped me. Trying to reason with him was impossible. After a while I realized I had to get away from him. As we were driving down the road, I jumped out of the moving car and ran across a field to get away. He shot me three times, one in the foot and two in the head. I knew this would be the end if I didn't do something fast. But what? The only thing I could do was to curl up on the ground and pray.

I called out to God and He heard my prayers. We always read in God's Word about the right hand of God. Well this day I felt the hand of God cover me and save me from the last bullets he had in his gun. He could do no more harm to me, because the God of heaven was listening and answered my prayers. I literally felt God's presence.

I thought I had gotten saved when I was twelve years old, but that day I was truly saved and I knew beyond a doubt it was God at work. While lying on the ground begging God for my life to be spared, I knew this was what rock bottom felt like. I could hear Him telling me, "Stay calm, I've got you."

This man later on committed more crimes against my parents and my family. Had it not been for the grace and mercy of God, I would not be alive to share my story now. This story stands as a warning to others who may be in the same situation I was in. Never, ever underestimate the power and the love of God. He tells us in His Word, *"My son, forget not my law; but let thine heart keep my commandments: For length of days, and long life, and peace, shall they add to thee"* (Proverbs 3:1-2).

—*Rebecca Armstrong*

CHAPTER 23
A Journey of Faith

A South Carolina woman credits Norton Cancer Institute for lifesaving care. I truly feel God put me in Dr. Lye's hands for a reason. He saved my life and I am so grateful to him and the team at Norton Cancer Institute.

In January 2024, I was feeling worn down and short of breath and experiencing a persistent cough. I was 78 years old and was normally full of life and constantly on the go, but now it took all I had to maintain my daily routine. I was bouncing between doctors in Greenville, South Carolina, but not getting answers. My health was failing quickly and my family feared the worst.

My son, Larry, and Dr. Lye are sports fathers – their kids play on the same sports teams in school. It was through this connection that Larry reached out to Dr. Lye and we decided I needed to be seen at Norton Cancer Institute.

On January 29 me and my husband, Ollie, began the road trip from South Carolina to Louisville. The week ahead of me was filled with appointments to see Dr. Lye, lab work, a biopsy and diagnostics like an MRI and PET scans. By that Friday Dr. Lye had discovered the root of the problem. I had stage IV lung cancer.

There was a mass in my lung that needed to be reduced in size before further action could be taken. Dr. Lye was waiting on the pathology of my tumor that would help him determine the treatment plan. This test could take another week for results, and Dr. Lye didn't feel they could wait that long.

Dr. Lye said my health was rapidly declining, so we arranged for me to start chemotherapy on the following Tuesday. Our goal was to start treatment and see if we could make an impact on the mass.

Fortunately, the pathology report came back in record time. The day before the chemo was to start Dr. Lye called me and my family with the news.

He said inside my mass was a specific mutation that could be treated with an oral medication. The medication attacks genetic mutations within the cancer cells that prove to be more effective with fewer side effects when compared to traditional chemotherapy. Thankfully it worked on me.

I was well enough to return home to Greenville by the following weekend and ten weeks after starting the medication, my follow-up PET scan showed I was cancer free! Today I maintain cancer care with Dr. Richard O'Neal. Dr. Lye stays in contact to manage my remission.

We continue to make trips back to Louisville, but instead of doctors' appointments, lab work and x-rays, we head to baseball and field hockey games to watch my grandchildren play or to Larry's home for family celebrations!

The Bible reminds us, *"He giveth strength to the weary and increases the power of the weak"* (Isaiah 40:29).

—*Cheryln Sanders Bradsher*

106

CHAPTER 24

The Apple of God's Eye

I did not see this coming….

When I was 39 years old, had two teenage daughters and of all things, we bought a childcare center! What possessed us to get into the childcare business only God knows for sure. The opportunity came and we took it. When we opened we had around 15 children from birth to 12 years. We closed in 2009 with 85 children. We were in business for 22 years and had the time of our lives.

The children had many stories to tell too. And believe me we heard them all. Don't let anyone tell you that children are not precious and precocious at the same time. We should realize that children are the apple of God's eye. Here are a few of our interactions that filled up our days….

It was a warm spring morning and just the day before we had the center carpets cleaned. As the children were being dropped off, I cautioned each one of them to wipe their feet off or take their shoes off so we could keep our carpet clean. I explained how it was costly to clean them. They all obliged just because they wanted to run around in their socks.

Periodically we would have unannounced DSS inspections and this day unfortunately was one of them. As the inspector came in the door one of our resident two-year-olds yells out to her, *"Take your shoes off before you come in. We just had the carpets cleaned and we don't have the money to clean them every day!"* The inspector was laughing so hard she almost cried. She even took her shoes off. She thought this was hilarious. I didn't!

Every day we tried to have a Bible story for the children. One day I read the story of Jacob and Esau. I was explaining how they were brothers, but they sometimes didn't get along with one another. I told how one brother had tricked the other. At the end I always asked questions about each story and at the end of the week those who knew the answers would get a prize. I happened to ask the question about Jacob and Esau. My question was what were the names of the brothers who just couldn't get along with each other. One little three-year-old answered my question. His answer was, *"Their names were Jacob and Pine-Sol."* He most definitely got a prize!

The final story I'll mention is our drink machine. This machine sat in our front foyer of the building between the two and three-year-old rooms. The drinks were for the adults and sold for 50 cents each. Every so often parents would send money for their child to buy a drink. One day a new child was attending his first day at school. As other children were getting their drink, he didn't know to bring money so I gave him the money for a drink. That night he went home and told his daddy he needed money to buy him a 50-cent drink. Not sure what he was talking about the dad came to me the next day and asked what is a 50-cent drink? I told him the kids had always called them 50-cent drinks so the name stuck. They never just said a Coke or a Fanta or a Sprite, but a 50-cent drink. They were called this until the day we closed. We sometimes remember the 50-cent drinks and ask for one even now!

This story is dedicated to children everywhere. You never know what they will say or do at any given time. If you're fortunate enough to be parents, love them to the fullest and enjoy their special moments with them. Here's a few words of parental advice: Don't say anything you don't want repeated. Don't fight in front of them, unless you want the whole world to know. Don't drink anything in front of them that you don't want others to know about. And whatever you do, don't break a promise! They grow up too fast. Before you know it they are grown and have children of their own. Make time to play and *listen* to what they have to say. You just might be surprised at what you'll learn. They are precious to us and more so to God.

He says, *"Keep my commandments and live; and my law as the apple of thine eye"* (Proverbs 7:2).

— *Kathy Lark*

CHAPTER 25
On Wings of Love

Today as I was cutting the grass in the field, I noticed this little robin following me. Everywhere I went in the field it would fly to me. I had to leave to go pick up Jace, my grandson, from school. When I got back my plan was to cut the front yard.

I went to the backyard to get the rider and when I went back around to the front, there was my little robin in the middle of the yard.

I've heard all my life about when red birds visit it means you are getting a visit from a loved one who has passed. Me, being curious, I had to google what it meant. It actually means that your loved one is at peace and is there watching over you. I so needed this today. I know God sent that little bird just for me. I feel sure Tony, my recently deceased husband, was watching over me. I know Tony is gone, but he'll never be forgotten! God's Word says, *"Look at the birds of the air, for they neither sow nor reap nor gather into barns, and yet your heavenly Father feeds them"* (Matthew 6:26).

— *Rita Kelly*

CHAPTER 26
A Bird Called Polly

I have experienced several miracles in my life. They stand out today as much as when they happened. God has been good to me and I know He's watching over me.

My first miracle occurred when I was fourteen and was a freshman in high school. One day I started not feeling too well and went to the school nurse. I called my mom and dad and asked them to come and pick me up. My dad was the one who came and got me. I went home and laid down on our couch while my mom and dad finished cleaning their room.

At the time we had a blue crowned conure parrot called Polly. All of a sudden Polly started making a strange, loud noise that alerted my parents that something was wrong. They ran into the living room where I had lain down and quickly realized I was having a seizure.

Had it not been for Polly, I wouldn't be here today. God works in many ways to protect us and this day Polly was the means He chose for me.

My second miracle was when I was a senior in high school. I was preparing to go to work after school. As I was finishing up my chest began to hurt. My mom rushed home and immediately took me to the hospital where I was almost in cardiac arrest.

The doctor prescribed a medicine for cardiac arrest patients that the nurse did not want to administer. He insisted and explained that if I didn't get it, I would die. Again, if it wasn't for God and my doctor, I could be gone today.

He spared my life on both occasions. I owe Him all the glory! God encourages us to pray these words, *"I will say of the Lord, He is my refuge and my fortress: my God; in him will I trust"* (Psalm 91:2).

—*Kasi Kelly*

CHAPTER 27
Extraordinary Days

Just weeks before this book went to the printers I had an extraordinary experience that put me in the hospital for three days and two nights. After transplant 10 years ago, I developed AFib and periodically had to go to the emergency room to get the episodes to stop. This story is about one of the trips.

The time was 2:30 am on June 5, 2025, when I awoke with an a-fib episode beginning. I immediately took all the prescribed medicines and laid back down to try and get the episode to pass. After about 2 hours it began to go away and I fell back to sleep.

Feeling better the next morning I got ready and went on to work. Around 9:30 I began to feel really bad and in a few moments' time I felt terrible. I felt like I was going to pass out and became really sick to my stomach. I felt so bad that I seemed to fade in and out of reality. Not being sure exactly what was going on I thought about calling my daughters to get them to come pick me up. I really wasn't sure if I could even make the call.

In what had to have been a miracle from God at that moment my phone rang. As I glanced over at the phone I saw that it was Christi, my oldest daughter, and knew that she never calls me in the morning. There must be a problem. In slow speech and complete fog I told her what was happening with me. She hung up and called my youngest daughter, and she came and drove me to the emergency room. Christi promised to meet us there since Andrea was much closer to me than she was at the time.

Andrea came and we drove to the hospital. I barely remember going there and still don't remember much until later in the emergency room. The triage nurse had just come on duty and assessed the situation and sent me immediately to the back.

In a short time my room was full of people. Several doctors and nurses working in a critical mode started lifesaving measures to fix my problem. My blood pressure was extremely low and my blood oxygen was 31. Never had I had this experience before and I hope never again.

The doctors and nurses at Greer Memorial Hospital were the best I have ever had in an emergency situation that could have gone really bad.

I was later admitted in the ICU and stayed for two nights for observation. They gradually restarted my medicines and all has been okay since.

While in the ICU one of the nurses was talking with me and she casually said to me. "You know if your daughter hadn't just 'happened' to call on the phone at the time she did, this could have had a whole lot different ending?" She then said, "God was watching out for you!" I told her about this book being written and how it was going to be printed soon. We both talked about how every day God is watching over us and when we least expect it, He is there!

I believe that God places angels in our lives in the form of friends, doctors, nurses, caregivers and family to help us when we can't help ourselves. He certainly did this for me that day.

Since then I have had a heart ablation and thanks to God, Dr. Peter Netzler, plus other good nurses and doctors, AFib is gone!

We don't know what tomorrow will bring. God sends us people who bless us and remind us of what He's doing for us continually. My nurse, Mindy, was a good example of a God moment in my life. She was there with words of encouragement and a reminder that even though I was expecting an ordinary day, God was sending an extraordinary one.

— *Kathy Lark*

God's word reminds us, *"My grace is sufficient for thee: for my strength is made perfect in weakness"* (II Corinthians 12:9).

Made in the USA
Middletown, DE
24 November 2025

21335420R00066